BY DEREK O'NEILL
Consciousness

Copyright © 2017 by Derek O'Neill

For information about permission to reproduce excerpts from this book write to:
Derek O'Neill
244 5th Avenue, Suite D-264
New York, NY 10001
E-Mail: info@derekoneill.com

ISBN: 978-1-936470-91-4
First Edition

All rights reserved, including the right to reproduce this work in any form whatsoever (audio, visual, electronic, etc.). Such reproduction is expressly forbidden without permission in writing from Derek O'Neill, except for brief passages in connection with a review. It is not the intent of the author to offer advice in any form, whether it is spiritual, psychological, medical, or other. If you are in need of special assistance or advice, please consult with a proper professional. The information within this book is offered as an avenue to inspiration and awareness. This book does not claim to possess all the answers, nor to heal or counsel. If you choose to apply the principles within this book to your life, that is your constitutional right.

Get a Grip Series © 2017
Editor: Nancy Moss
Front Cover Design: Derek O'Neill

DEDICATION

To all who read this book, I salute you for wanting to change the way you live for the better and for having the courage to be who you are as fully as possible.

To all who encourage me every day to keep going and sharing their lives with me, family small and large. But most of all the little angels who came to teach me – Alexa, Blake and Calvin, my grandchildren.

"Everybody hurts sometimes, and when we do it is nice to have Derek O'Neill around. His excellent little books on the things that get us, (fear, anger, depression, victimhood, mental blocks) allow us to find our way safely through our psychological minefields and arrive safely at the other side. Read them when you need them."

Paul Perry, Author of the
New York Times Bestseller
Evidence of the Afterlife

TABLE OF CONTENTS

Author's Preface..*ix*

What Is Consciousness? 1

Changing Consciousness – Creating Your Reality 8

How the Monkey Mind Affects Your Consciousness 17

Positive Consciousness 23

Generational Consciousness & Karma ..30

How Our Personal Consciousness Affects Collective Consciousness 36

The Battle of Consciousness in the Bhagavad Gita 42

Higher Consciousness, Higher Power ..48

Meditation..52

Practical Exercises for Understanding and Tapping into Consciousness 56

About The Author..*67*

AUTHOR'S PREFACE

Thank you for purchasing *Consciousness: It's All Over You*. This book has not come about as a result of my training as a therapist, but through some hard-earned lessons that I have experienced myself. This is how I know the path out of limiting beliefs and behaviors that hinder growth. The tools that I offer in this book have worked not only for me, but also for hundreds if not thousands of other people. I have shared these ideas and techniques in my workshops, one-on-one sessions, video and radio broadcasts, and on my website, and I have witnessed astounding results time and time again. Through observation of others, and myself, I have learned to identify the triggers and root causes of disharmony. Most of all, I have come to understand and apply the best methods for achieving peace and balance in life; not perfection, but real transformation and harmony that comes with learning who we are and what makes us tick. My 35 years of martial arts study has given me a refined sense of timing for when to strike with the sword to cut away old patterns, and when to use the brush to paint the picture of the life we deserve and can have.

The 'Get a Grip' series of books offers tangible, authentic wisdom that can help you in all aspects of your life. You've made a great choice by investing in this book. Enjoy the read, and take time to learn and apply the techniques. Let's change who we are together.

Derek

Consciousness

It's All Over You

WHAT IS CONSCIOUSNESS?

The Three Levels of Consciousness

What is the meaning of "consciousness"? Where does it come from and how does it shape our lives? There's the scientific view of consciousness which looks at details of the brain and its functions. Consciousness is also defined as our thinking, our perceptions, our system of beliefs and spirituality, and the entirety of our self-reflection. Though our reality seems dependent on what our external world looks like – where we live, our relationships, our economic situation, etc. – in truth, it's our consciousness that creates our reality and determines what the external world is serving up at any given time.

The manifestation of your state of mind – your consciousness – influences your life in every conceivable way. Your consciousness will always be a stronger force than the external world around you. No matter how potentially jarring or seemingly powerful a life-changing episode can feel, your consciousness will create your reaction. Life is a pendulum that swings back and forth, from pleasure to pain, from darkness to light; we choose which one we want to experience at any given time. Your consciousness determines your reality. Your goals are to be aware of your consciousness and how to shift it, the role it plays in the various scenarios life presents to you, and how your individual consciousness affects the collective consciousness (and vice versa). When we attain a higher consciousness, we achieve perspective and the inner truth that helps us understand, accept, and love ourselves so we can be aware in every moment.

Think of consciousness as the blueprint of your mind. That blueprint is sitting there, waiting for you to acknowledge it so that you find your passion in life. Consciousness is continually manifesting your world on more than one level. To launch us into the topic, let's look at how consciousness exists on three levels.

The first level, "the conscious mind," encompasses your thinking, feelings, and reactions, as they happen in real time. The conscious mind is what you are reading with right now. In simplest terms, it's being awake and aware that there is a "self" that you experience the world through. Consciousness knows right and wrong – usually – and it is the mind that is most active during your day. This includes thinking about the past and the future on a conscious level. Consciousness arises from a connection to the mind that exists in the present and focuses on the creation of new possibilities at any given moment. When our consciousness is intentional and aware, it leads us into deeper self-reflection, and allows us to relate to other people with compassion as we recognize we are all one, each a part of the whole.

The second level is the "subconscious mind." Think about the subconscious as the mind that lies underneath. It affects your consciousness in a powerful way as it has imprinted experiences that have happened in your life – that you may or may not be aware of – but that play an important role in how they affect your current consciousness. The subconscious could be called the paintbox of your mind, coloring your thoughts and sketching your perceptions. It is a library of every event you have ever experienced, that is now subtly influencing who you are and how you process your present life experiences. Understanding the subconscious, and how it shapes your conscious mind, can shed light on old patterns of behavior and belief systems, as well as your ability to accept and change your ways of thinking for the better. The subconscious knows everything about us. Our journey is to lovingly open up its multitude of "files" and embrace how we got to this point in life. With the subconscious' help, we can stop the struggle we experience within certain areas of our lives.

The third level of consciousness is our "higher consciousness." We could also refer to it as our "superconsciousness" or "overriding consciousness." Some people call this level of consciousness the "Higher Self"," "Source," or "the God-self." The higher consciousness acts as a neutral force on both the positive and the negative poles that are created by the conscious and subconscious minds. When a neutral force acts upon positive and negative forces, a spark-like energy is created that inspires wisdom, creativity, even genius. The superconsciousness observes and acknowledges a higher plane of existence that can help make sense of the chaos and provide a unifying path to acceptance and happiness. The more your consciousness grows, the more you understand yourself, and everything and everyone around you.

The topic of consciousness is rich and far-reaching. Many cultures, philosophies, and belief systems offer teachings that can illuminate a fascinating exploration into our very being. For example, Buddhist teachings offer nine levels of consciousness, which expands on the three I've outlined above. The first five levels encompass the use of our senses – the consciousness of what we see, hear, smell, touch and taste. We don't all experience these levels the same way from day-to-day or person-to-person, because our belief systems create filters that alter our perceptions. Mindfulness, when it comes to our senses, puts us in conscious contact with our surroundings. This can lead to a greater sense of wholeness and appreciation. The 6th through 8th levels in Buddhism lead up to the subconscious level where the blueprint of your life and its karma resides. The 9th level is pure consciousness and enlightenment which is accessed through teachings and meditation and is the highest rung of the superconscious.

Ultimately, consciousness is energy. By bringing together the three levels of consciousness, we can shift and change that energy. In the pages that follow, you will begin to have a deeper understanding about consciousness, and how you can change it for greater happiness, peace and a deeper connection to Source.

CHANGING CONSCIOUSNESS – CREATING YOUR REALITY

How do we truly change what seems to make us unhappy? How many times have you tried to bring about change by attempting to alter external circumstances, without shifting your consciousness about it? Do you try to control your world instead of your mind? Change begins with a process of thoughts, words, and actions – and our ability to bring consciousness into our daily lives. If we change our thoughts, words and actions, our reality changes. This is the only way to create change for individuals and for the world.

There is a saying that goes, "A man whose thoughts, words and actions are in alignment can never be vexed by anger."

The same follows for any emotion or event that, on its surface, disrupts our happiness. So where do thoughts come from? Our thoughts come from our conscious mind. Where do our words come from? Our words come from experience; a word is something recalled from a memory. We remember words and we put those words into patterns to express what it is we are trying to achieve or say. Our subconscious shows up in our words, even if we are not aware of its influence. The more we understand about our subconscious, the more we can use words to our benefit. For example, if our child does something that we were yelled at for doing by *our* parents, our subconscious may very well react in a way that channels the hurt we felt and we end up using the same action and words with our child. Or we could find ourselves becoming defensive when someone makes a suggestion to us, because our subconscious remembers feeling hurt and powerless when a boss gave us a harsh review. When we bring the subconscious into the light, we break patterns and vicious cycles of unhappiness and pain.

Where do our actions come from? Our actions are the result of how aware – or unaware – we are, whether our conscious and subconscious have a connection between them, and if we know how to act from a higher level of intention. Our actions should be the result of the thoughts and the words we choose. We have control over them. Actions that don't arise from conscious intention of thoughts and words are too often a reaction in the moment, that doesn't represent who you are aspiring to be, but instead who you were, when you were operating from your old belief systems. If we begin to align thoughts, words, and actions in the moment with conscious intention, a super/higher consciousness evolves naturally.

The superconscious mind just sits and watches the play between the conscious and subconscious. It watches humanity grasp at materialistic wealth, fame and power, and sees us becoming more and more frustrated because the chase for happiness comes up empty. The role of the superconscious in our daily life is like a mother who is sitting, waiting for her child to come and ask, "Is it safe to do this?" "Is it safe to let go, and look for something more meaningful?" It is the all-knowing, all-experiencing part of who we are that knows absolutely, without a doubt, the ultimate truth of right and wrong. Our conscious mind gives us versions of right and wrong, our subconscious mind holds the blueprint of how we became who we are, and the super/higher conscious gives us a way to change.

The universe wants you to be happy. That may surprise you, but it's true. At its core, your consciousness is pure and neutral. It carries the blueprint of who you are, and its purity with higher level of thinking is always there to tap into. We choose whether or not to allow the universe to just give us what it naturally wants to, the best for our highest good and the good of one and all. Your consciousness' default is as pure as the driven snow – it's you that tips it either one way or the other. Your lack of awareness and knowledge, leading to either positive or negative patterns of thoughts or actions, defines how the universe will respond. Once you see consciousness as the most important thing you can control, you can start to change your life. Your mind is what shifts; the external world is just the mirror to the main stage of your consciousness.

If you've ever made a deliberate effort to smile for a day or even a few hours, you've probably noticed the difference in how your world makes a subtle shift. We may not have felt like there was anything in particular to smile about, but we can "fake it 'till we make it." When you smile, the endorphins shoot into your body and calmness and positivity kick in. It's the same concept we can use to change bigger and more long-term elements of our life. Through understanding and connecting with consciousness, we do not have to wait for things to change on the outside, all we need is to tap into our inner consciousness and we can find the source of the behavior causing the issue.

Using the knowledge of our different levels of consciousness, the sense-thinking level, the one we call "consciousness," benefits from being more mindful. If we start a program of change there, where we are more deliberate in what we see and hear and feel, our consciousness sharpens and focuses. Once you are more aware of what you are doing, the space you are inhabiting, the conversations you have with people, your breathing as you walk, the sound of a child playing, a reaction you have to a story you read, etc. – you are opening the door for further growth and transformation. We cannot change if we are unaware. Too often we go through the motions of our day without noticing much. Mindfulness makes consciousness its partner. Being consciously mindful should come about naturally. Sometimes, being aware and conscious can be painful when we are avoiding certain realities. Humans distract themselves, or zone out, to avoid what is unpleasant. It's no surprise that we are wired that way. But tapping into consciousness is a way to stop "kicking the can" so to speak, pushing away feelings that will only come back stronger if we don't find a way to confront and accept them. This is where awareness and connection with the subconscious comes into the process of self-realization and change.

When we understand what it means and feels like to be "conscious" we can start the process of bringing the subconscious out of hiding and into the light where we can acknowledge and learn from it. It can be challenging to access your subconscious mind but when the conscious and subconscious connects, you become healthy in spirit, mind, and body. There is a term in psychology called the "critical factor", or the "critical mind", which is another name for ego. Using the critical mind/ego will allow you to practice self-analysis and self-introspection. Often, a teacher can help guide you because the critical mind will begin to lie to your conscious mind about how good you are or are not. This is when you need the objective, nonjudgmental force of an inner (the superconscious or higher conscious aspect of self) or an outer teacher, to apply neutral insights on the positive and negative experiences of your life. The higher consciousness holds the understanding and love of acceptance quite literally, it is a "higher" view of ourselves and what we have experienced or are going through in the present. The higher consciousness sees the bigger picture of both our individual journey and all of humankind as an integrated whole. The superconscious lives both inside us and in the universe. It marries all three levels of consciousness into what life means right now. When we become clear and truthful enough, we can do this ourselves, otherwise an external teacher is suggested to help us see what we are blind to, based on old belief systems adopted from our prior experiences.

HOW THE MONKEY MIND AFFECTS YOUR CONSCIOUSNESS

The monkey mind is always looking to invade your consciousness. It's the mind of worry, fear, anxiety and desire. The monkey mind grasps at what you think you need to feel happy, safe and secure. It chatters away in your head, in an endless cycle that – if you cling to it – will always have you in its grip. The monkey mindset can become so ingrained in our consciousness, that we lose sense of perspective and higher truth. It is a narrow lens that we see ourselves and the world through, blocking out all the possibility for growth and joy.

The term "monkey mind" is based on how, in India, there are many monkey tribes that roam around and steal food from people. In order to stop them, the people make big, heavy clay jugs with a narrow neck that they place fruit in. When the monkeys come around and put their hand into the jar to grab the fruit, they can't get their hand back out of the jar because they won't let go of the fruit. That is exactly what many of us are doing in our lives. We keep grabbing stuff we think we own, or that we think is going to make us happy or secure and we don't let go, thus becoming trapped in a thought process, an old belief about ourselves or how our life should be. There's nothing in life that will stay the same. There are no guarantees, except the one that everything will change. If our consciousness partners with the monkey mind, it will grasp onto what we need not hold any longer, old beliefs. If we don't accept impermanence and uncertainty into our consciousness, we'll be stuck, just like a hand in a narrow-necked jar. We must reflect on and understand the workings of our subconscious mind and let go of what we mistakenly created as truth. That delusion is the source of our feeling crazy and/or miserable now.

Letting go of the monkey mind begins with identifying it. Look at everything that's going on around you. There's no coincidence in what you are experiencing in your life right now – everything is happening to show you something. Once you are conscious of this, you can know what you are meant to push through, and what you are meant to let go of. But you won't know until you can sit still. As we bring consciousness into a much more important place in our world, everything that was familiar to us begins to drop away. The analytical process drops away. The old ways of doing business drop away. The best advice anybody can receive is to let the monkey mind go and see what takes its place. If you want to stop doing something in your life that causes suffering to yourself or to another, you're going to have to consciously identify it. You're going to have to look at the subconscious and where your actions come from. That's what gives you the foundation to reach a higher consciousness.

The monkey mind tells your consciousness that life is a constant race between "winning" and "losing," and that you are defined by how much you have under "control" in your external life. In truth, there's nothing to be gained and there's nothing to be lost, and you don't really have "control" over anything, it is an illusion. We're all going to the same place. What's the use of grasping that which cannot be grasped? It only leads to suffering and won't allow your consciousness to expand.

What is the best way to quiet the monkey mind and connect with consciousness? Learn to react with neutrality to all that arrives in your life and become detached to the outcome. You don't do it, it comes through you naturally when you sit in grace and become its vibration. Meditation is a wonderful avenue to this goal. It takes discipline and determination, which means making it a daily practice. It is being consciously aware of your thought process. When you are in "conscious contact" with all that is around you, and the different levels of consciousness within you are being processed, this allows the monkey mind to quiet down. Be kind with yourself on this journey; know that these patterns can be hardwired into our psyches. It takes work and commitment to ease your consciousness into a more enlightened state. There is no rule or expectation of how long it takes to get there, or even what path you need to take. The most important thing is that you use awareness and connection to consciousness as your light. If you chase after a result, the energy of the monkey mind and desire push away what you are looking for. Grasping for a result or an outcome will only block progress.

Return to the concept of "thoughts, words and actions." When your monkey mind starts its noise, come back to the conscious present. What are you feeling? Take notice of your physical and mental space. What in the subconscious could be connected to these feelings? What are the words that those feelings conjure? How can you best express your inner feelings? What actions can you take, with conscious intent, to change the negative emotions and thought patterns, and manifest a reality based on how you see the world? Life is always serving up opportunities for you to let go of the monkey mind and walk a path to higher consciousness. No matter how mired down in challenges you may be at certain points in your life, you can ALWAYS turn around the way you are viewing your journey.

POSITIVE CONSCIOUSNESS

As much as we know that our thoughts – whether positive or negative – will affect our feelings and manifest our reality, it is often difficult to keep up the positive mindset in the face of events or situations that arise. We need to look at our thinking from a perspective of consciousness. It is only with this deeper dive into our psyche, and blueprint of who we are, that we can adopt a long-term positive effect. It's not only about recognizing your patterns. It's about understanding that a mind will create a story. Whether that story is true or not can only be decided by you, and you alone. With so much emphasis on the physical world, the power of consciousness is overlooked. We often focus on the circumstances in our lives that aren't going well, instead of thinking about what is going well and counting our blessings. We focus on what we see as problematic, instead of looking at the bigger picture and all who are involved in it.

Positive consciousness starts with the awareness of the ability of your mind to change and grow. Consciousness is the most powerful tool in breaking the negative emotions that can cause a chain reaction in our brains. Utilizing a conscious decision to turn over these feelings to a higher level of consciousness and let them go is not easy, it takes consistent minute-by-minute work. When we persist, we begin to see the expansive nature of consciousness, as opposed to the "small mind" focus on our problems. Then the picture of our lives and the outer experiences begin to change, and then the bigger definition adjusts. Positive consciousness acknowledges negative thoughts and feelings but doesn't hold on to them. Positive consciousness is in partnership with the subconscious, which understands why our mind tends to default to the negative. We may have heard "don't" and "can't" and "not" much more in the past than "go for it" and "you can do it" and "yes". Our higher consciousness defaults to positive so much so that it does not hear negatives in sentences. When we say, "I am not smoking again", our mind only hears, "I am smoking again" – it takes out the "not" because that's a negative and it blocks out negatives. There might have been a purpose of basic survival, back when we were emerging as humans, to hear the negative warnings of lurking danger, and that's why society carried those negative statements forward. We have now evolved to higher purposes – to ourselves and to the world – that point to positivity needing to be our default in what we say and do. It is not only possible but necessary. Both individuals and the entire planet are helped by positive consciousness.

The next step in positive consciousness is the realization that positivity is acutely closer to "neutrality" than we may think. To keep a positive mindset is more about accepting the ebb and flow of life rather than forcing an unnatural brightness. When we keep our consciousness in the positive realm, we are greeting ALL that life encompasses with a "hello," and a "welcome." We greet joy the same as pain; birth the same as death. Emotions are embraced, whether they be sadness or happiness, and we are not scared of any of these emotions, nor do we hold on to them as if they will never change. Everything will change around us. Internally, our consciousness can bring peace and a sense of continuity by being neutral and nonjudgmental. Positive consciousness is nurtured by receiving life on the universe's terms, not ours.

Consciousness can too often be stuck in a cycle of aversion and attachment. Your mind is the cause of aversion and attachment.

Something that starts off pleasant may end up being very unpleasant. Like eating a tub of ice cream. It begins well, tasting good and giving you pleasure, but as you finish off the whole thing, then wolf down a second tub, and then a third, what started off as sweet has turned unappetizing and painful. Within every aversion there is an attachment, and within every attachment there is an aversion. The transient nature of everything means that we cannot hold on to any of it. It will all come and it will all go. If we are attached, we are setting ourselves up for sorrow. All the things we think are important are a delusion. As we look past our former definitions of what had defined us, we discover who we really are – a part of the bigger consciousness. We will only be happy if we let go of what we hold onto in the outer world and strive for a higher consciousness in the inner world. There is nothing wrong with having material things, or enjoying people or places, it is our attachment to them that causes us to suffer.

If only we were always in a state of equilibrium and balance, it would be easy to see that everything is in divine accord, and all that occurs externally happens in Divine Order. The fact is, we're not! We are creating our own reality by how our consciousness reacts to life, whether it be good fortune, or misfortune. There's nothing wrong with being attracted to pleasure by directing your consciousness towards it, as long as you know that the space between two pleasures is pain, and conversely the space between two pains is pleasure. So sooner or later, pleasure is going to demanifest. The evolution of consciousness, and the goal that teachings and meditations reach for, is neutrality. This is the higher consciousness that yogis have – the ability to neutralize the whole game. That's why they can sit perfectly still. They're neither attracted to pleasure nor averted by pain.

They just are, and that's what we should be doing, as best as we can. When we are neutral we are not attracted to nor averted by anything, we just accept it for what it is and we act in the moment. The enlightenment of a higher consciousness is not something you go looking for – you are it, already. Look inside yourself and let the universe do its thing. We don't create a superconscious, we already have it, we just get rid of the blocks – the negative thinking, the desires, the need to control – that keep it from being revealed. You may not have the answer to all the questions the universe and life poses, yet through meditation you do have access to all the answers. Ask and you shall receive, but first you have to ask. This is the enlightenment that's available to you right now. Enjoy it!

GENERATIONAL CONSCIOUSNESS & KARMA

We know we are affected by our past, and that the baggage our parents carried in their lives seeped into the way we were raised. Looking back through the generations, we see a chain of dynamics that – though manifested differently at each stage in a family – are alive and kicking through time. We can call it generational consciousness or karma, and it plays out in everyone's life. Some belief systems are so buried in the subconscious, that we are not even aware of them. Even if we are aware of what happened in our families, going back two or three generations, it can be hard to know how to learn from this karma and change the tide moving forward. There could be pain and suffering in your family from many generations ago that has been brought forward for you to deal with. The way you were raised, talked to, loved or not loved, has been brought forward in belief systems you adopted because of those experiences. Understanding generational consciousness is a journey that brings together our conscious knowledge and our ability to tap into our subconscious to explore and accept the influences of the things we have experienced. It is only by becoming conscious of our thoughts and thought patterns that we can begin to connect with the karma we were born into and shift its effect.

Let's use the example of a father who has an issue with anger. This might have been the result of him being neglected or abandoned by his parents, or some other trauma. You recognize anger in your own life; the way you react to things, or maybe how you push people away who make you feel vulnerable. That anger will grow and fester, perhaps even showing up as physical illness, unless you address the consciousness around it. When we feel victimized by the karma that arrives for us, we tend to feed it instead of understanding it and letting it go. You have to take back your power from your father or whomever it is in your family/past that you've adopted these behavior patterns from. You must look at what triggers an emotional response in you, and you will see how they relate to this generational karma and the belief systems you bought into as a child. We pass our "stuff" on in life and the majority of the time we're passing it on unconsciously. You can see it when you lose your temper at your child, or snap at someone at work. Imagine if your daughter was singing and you came home, feeling grumpy and angry. You yell at her to "shut up" and now you've crushed her spirit to sing, and her dream. If she carries resentment moving forward, she's likely to pass it on to her children.

We all have bad moments that are not deliberate, but we need to get to a space at some stage where we look at these moments and see them for what they are. Otherwise, this generational consciousness continues for the next generation and beyond. I absolutely believe that anybody willing to work with an open mind on understanding and shifting their consciousness can break the patterns of their karma, many generations back, and many generations forward. No matter what you carry from your family – abuse, addiction, etc. – if you see your connection to it you can break those chains. It's a mistake to see yourself as separate from it. You may not be the abuser or the alcoholic, but you are actually one with them in terms of karma. This is how you stop the chain reaction of this consciousness to the next generation. You've thought of yourself as separate in order to protect yourself, which was the right thing to do, yet there comes a time in adulthood when you have to see it for what it is, and let it go. I cannot change anyone else, and neither can you. But you can change yourself in a second. It's a flip in consciousness.

Your karmic seeds are playing a role in producing a reality that you don't want. It's important to understand and accept that – it's like a potter's wheel that started a long time ago and it's still in motion. The way you react to it is what creates your future. Events of the past are bearing down on your consciousness. You're not only dealing with what you did in your life, but in your past life, and in your family's karmic life. If that is impacting you, it's easy to neutralize by saying, "Thank you, I created that! I am the cause, here are the subconscious effects within me that I now release going forward."

Don't get caught up in the wheels that go on, and on, and on. Remember, ultimately it is your mind that creates your reality. Look at the opportunity you are being given to change the patterns of your consciousness. This can transform the generational karma, and stop anger, misunderstanding, and abuse from affecting your children, and others close to you.

HOW OUR PERSONAL CONSCIOUSNESS AFFECTS COLLECTIVE CONSCIOUSNESS

What is the "collective consciousness?" How is it created? How can it benefit our world, and when is our personal consciousness a part of that? When individuals work on understanding their consciousness, and start living a more mindful life, they are contributing to a higher consciousness that impacts others positively. Collective consciousness is a powerful gathering of thought, vision and energy that can create change – on both a small and large scale. Awareness and action on issues, locally and globally, find their roots in collective consciousness. At the end of the day, we are all connected. We cannot separate ourselves from the idea of unity with the rest of the world, in all forms. That said, it's important to remember that your personal consciousness is where it starts and where your initial focus must be. There are times that the collective consciousness seems to be working against positive outcomes and could be a block for personal growth, that's when your ability to hold a positive consciousness is most needed. The world's collective consciousness at this moment is complicated. On one hand, there is a lot of fear, misunderstanding, grasping at material things, and negative mindsets. We can also see manifestations of hope, abundance in life, and connection. It is important that you bring your personal consciousness into alignment with people who are not in fear or drama, and hold a positive outlook for the collective consciousness going forward.

At this time in society and cultures worldwide, it's a societal subconscious that we need to heal. We can negate harmful consciousness when we begin with ourselves and our understanding of our subconscious as individuals, how it affects our daily lives, and our connection to others. Large consequences and change can begin with small steps. Think of it this way – unlimited consciousness can be brought down to the point of a needle. The power of that point on the needle head is greater than the whole collective consciousness of everything else. It works the other way also, that one small act of kindness can have a powerful, expansive result, radiating outward into the collective consciousness. Meditation is a vehicle for seeing this concept manifest. When you learn to meditate you lift up through your conscious, then up through your subconscious, and out into the superconscious. We also bring the personal consciousness into alignment with a positive collective consciousness when we gather together to learn and share. When we share our consciousness, we start to release the sources and patterns of thoughts and actions that cause a lot of the illness and sadness in our lives. As we release it, we also release it in everyone else's lives, that is the power of the collective consciousness – as we heal ourselves, all are healed. We can manifest an accepting, higher consciousness as individuals and as a group. Buddha said, "He who experiences the unity of life sees his own self in all beings, and all beings in his own self, and looks on everything with an impartial eye."

When we bring our personal consciousness together with others to form a collective consciousness, we see the power of manifestation in action. Service to others arises naturally when we understand the connection between the individual and the community. One of the best ways to heal your subconscious and attain a higher consciousness is to serve others. Many teachings address how enlightenment will come faster when you give of yourself generously. What action can you take that will make a difference to someone else? Manifestation happens very fast when you're doing it for the good of other people. When you're trying to manifest something in your own life, it's much slower. If you see someone suffering and you help them, your suffering begins to alleviate. Generosity is received and returned to you a millionfold. Service is not just a physical action, it is also holding positive consciousness for those in need. Consciousness is the awareness, knowledge and power to change lives.

Ultimately, each and every one of us are responsible for our own creation and for what has been created in the world, including the negative aspects we see. Collectively, we can reshape the collective consciousness on the planet now. We can help in many ways, especially by sharing from our higher consciousness that which speaks to hope and strength. That said, don't seek out suffering by listening to those around you who are negative about what is going on. You could be creating it by seeming to support it. The best form of service you can do at that moment is not to see the suffering, but rather, allow the compassion to arise in you as an act of service. Remember that everyone is on their own journey, and has to be willing to receive help. You cannot control other people's path, yet it's within your individual power, and our positive collective consciousness, to stop creating negative karma for ourselves and everyone in the world, by silently holding compassion for someone in a negative space or mindset.

THE BATTLE OF CONSCIOUSNESS IN THE BHAGAVAD GITA

Once we understand the basic concepts of consciousness, there are many teachings and texts that provide a deeper exploration into the topic. Some of the strongest expressions of consciousness can be found in spiritual writings that use metaphors to tell stories that reflect our internal battle with the external influences of the world. The Bhagavad Gita is an ancient Hindu text written by sages who broke through the universe's power of illusion and wrote a guidebook for us on how to live a God-realized life. It is called the devotees "Song of love to God."

The Bhagavad Gita is written in story form about a battle that took place in 317

BCE and is still taking place today in modern times. It is about who we really are, what we have really come to experience, and the different levels through which we have come to experience it in. It speaks as clearly to the person just starting out to learn about spirituality, as well as the person who has spent years on the spiritual path.

The main characters in the book are Arjuna, who represents humanity and devotion, and Krishna who represents the Godhead. It is a symbol of what we could call the original "Conversations with God," since Arjuna is meant to be us, talking to Krishna/God. Arjuna is faced with a moral dilemma in the story. He is the trained warrior of the family of the Pandavas, and he is facing off with his cousin, the trained warrior of the Kurus. The Kurus have stolen some property from the Pandavas and Arjuna is to fight them for it in a battle to the death, winner takes all. Arjuna asks Krishna to be his chariot driver and drive him onto the battlefield. When they get there, Arjuna sees those he has to fight. He becomes distraught and wants to give up. He doesn't want to kill his cousins, uncles, teachers, and friends. In fact, he says "death would be better" for him, and so he calls on Krishna for advice.

How does this relate to our lives today? When Arjuna asks Krishna to tell him what he should do, Krishna tells him a story that reflects what our true Dharma (right action/ moral conduct) is in life – and it is not necessarily what we have been led to believe life is about. Winning the battle is not about how successful you are in business, how much money you have in the bank, how great you look, or any of the other things society has falsely tried to convince us of.

Krishna tells Arjuna about where the battle is really being fought, it is being fought within us – in our consciousness. The time for the outer wars is over, now the real battle is within ourselves. It is a battle of consciousness between your good and bad senses, and you can either win the throne of senses or you can win the throne of wisdom. The Pandavas represent the good senses or spiritual wisdom, and the Kuru's represent the bad senses or mental desires. We have good desires and we have bad desires. The good desires are about using our senses to reach God (or a higher power) within us, the bad desires are using our senses to reach only for the earthly fruit – the 'fun' stuff we see around us – fame, success, money, etc.

The Bhagavad Gita portrays God as siting on his throne, watching how the players (us) play the game of life. The prize is to reach Him/Her/It. (I will use "He" from here on out, open to your interpretation…). He sees how and where we go to find Him, and the struggles we go through to avoid the pitfalls we encounter along the way to reach Him. To make it interesting of course, since it is a battle, He gives us weapons along the way to help us fight, along with little clues like spiritual books. He even throws in a teacher for us here and there, if we are lucky, to help us stay on the path. He gives us the Grace and the strength to climb the mountains that block us, that manifest as challenging experiences we need to overcome. And all the while God is holding the reigns of our senses and creating all the incidents along our path, so we can come home to Him. All we need to do is accept that we are on our way there.

The Bhagavad Gita shows us the age-old struggle that has been going on in people's lives forever. It recounts what others have done to overcome the struggle and drama, and win the battle. We learn about the "weapons" we can use like meditation, concentration and contemplation, the teachings we can embrace, and how we can find the courage to face the challenges in our lives. We can apply these elements to the consciousness we need to raise the kids, navigate relationships, find meaning in work, study, and to be in service to others. The Bhagavad Gita is a guidebook that tells us the choice is ours. It asks what choice are we going to make, and what is important to us. It is a map to get back to God/Higher Consciousness.

I encourage you to read more about the Bhagavad Gita as part of understanding consciousness and its application to your spiritual path.

HIGHER CONSCIOUSNESS, HIGHER POWER

If we think of higher or superconsciousness as something only attained by living the life of a yogi in a cave, we miss the opportunity to see how it is reachable to us, every day. There is a pure form of higher consciousness that takes a tremendous amount of immersion into teachings, along with separation from society's influences, but "regular" people can tap into a higher mindset. What people call their "higher power" comes in many forms. It can be a deity you have put your faith in, teachings you ascribe to, the universe and/or nature, or that part of your being which transcends time, place and situation. Upon seeing a "higher" answer to whatever you are thinking or experiencing, it can be a combination of all of these. It is also the end result of when we connect subconscious awareness to our daily consciousness. Higher consciousness is at the core of perspective, neutrality, acceptance, gratitude, service and positive thinking.

There are few people who exist in a perfect, blissful higher consciousness. Our challenge is to bring our consciousness back to a place of harmony with life-affirming energy and resilience. That said, it is not enough to take in teachings about higher consciousness or power, thinking you understand and that your life will magically transform. Whatever you learn about consciousness here or elsewhere must be backed up with devotion to your path. We are being greeted by the collective gathering of past and future karma every day of our lives, and every day is an opportunity to confront and change it. Gaining awareness and insight is just a start, you must put what you learn into practice by applying teachings and accepting life as a journey. Only those who have attained the purest form of higher consciousness have arrived at the destination. The rest of us are traveling there.

Turning your consciousness over to a higher power is not about letting go of personal responsibility. All that you perceive around you will disappear someday. Only consciousness survives. Everything you observe and feel is coming from your consciousness. When you smell a yellow rose, that yellow rose is not there for everybody on the planet. It is there for you alone. You have created it with your consciousness. You have chosen to see a rose where others might choose to see a weed. Your consciousness is creating your reality. Take responsibility for what you are manifesting in your life and your consciousness will begin to create rose gardens upon rose gardens, all without thorns.

MEDITATION

How Our Consciousness, Joined Together, Creates Healing for Everyone

In broad terms, consciousness could be called a meditation. Consciousness is all about focusing on thought, clearing the mind for neutrality, and achieving a higher level of perspective from the practice and application of how to shift our reality.

As you reach the end of this book, here is a meditation that quiets the mind and focuses on how our individual consciousness can come together and create healing in other people, and in the world. When we go deep into our consciousness and tap into its higher purpose, we can radiate out the energy that gathers in the collective consciousness. We need not be with the people we wish to send positivity or healing to – in fact we can be meditating in solitude. The power of one person's consciousness is interconnected with every living being and your energy can reach them, wherever they are – that's the collective consciousness.

****

Find a quiet place in your home, or join others in a meditation class or gathering. Close your eyes and concentrate on your breath. Clear your mind. If thoughts and feelings arise, greet them, then send them away for now. Your goal is balance and neutrality.

Scan your body, feeling the energy, starting with your toes, up your feet and legs, to your torso, out to your arms, then up through your neck to your head. Relax each part of your body as you focus on it. Once you've scanned your entire body, go back to concentrating on your breath. Your consciousness should feel open and receptive, allowing the energy you feel inside you, and around you, to connect you to this very moment.

Now focus on the energy of your heart. Feel the power of your consciousness concentrate in your heart. From there, imagine a bright light gathering in the center of your heart. Sit with that sensation, then imagine light radiating outwards.

While concentrating on the light, see it as consciousness in its purest form. Feel the connection between your heart and mind, shining the light between both. Now think of the consciousness of those around you (if you are meditating as a group) and/or people in your life. See the light envelope others. It is the same light that surrounds you.

Extend your concentration out to the room, then the building, the road, the town, etc., to the whole world. Focus on the collective consciousness. Feel the interconnectedness of the universe.

Take the collective energy of consciousness and think of the light as a healing beacon. Envelope your fellow meditators if with others, your friends and family, your community, the country, the world, and the universe in the positive, healing, radiant power of consciousness. Sit with the energy of interconnection and peace.

Slowly bring the light back to yourself, your heart and your mind. As you come out of the meditation, feel the consciousness of love and compassion – for yourself and others – as a gift and guide as you go about your day.

PRACTICAL EXERCISES FOR UNDERSTANDING AND TAPPING INTO CONSCIOUSNESS

The following are suggestions for thoughts and actions that can help shift your consciousness, get in touch with your subconscious, and begin to see life through the lens of a higher/superconsciousness.

- When something in your life changes (it can be slight or big), sit with your first reaction but then switch to another perspective. Ask yourself if there's another way to see this change? Look into what it is in your subconscious that may be influencing your feelings. Don't worry if you cannot sustain perspective and neutrality at all times; it is a process and a practice to shift consciousness. It is also not an avoidance of issues or actions you need to take. Rather it's a way to gain the calm, higher consciousness that will help you face any situation.

- Our mind can bring us down rabbit holes that are endless. Have you experienced the feeling that it is spinning endlessly? Here's how to stop the mind, if only for a minute! It's a great feeling that you can use as the basis for further work on clearing the mind and meditation: Close your eyes and ask yourself, "I wonder what my next thought is going to be? Your mind stops immediately, because it goes searching for the next thought, and completely leaves you alone and opens up a clearer space in your awareness.

- Practice staying in the moment, and don't get stuck in any particular mindset. Keep bringing the mind back to neutrality and the concept of impermanence. Grasping burdens our consciousness.

Greet events, take them in and feel your feelings. Then, let those feelings go. Depending on what they are, you may or may not revisit the emotions, but you will have practiced consciously shifting your perspective. Try this with small reactions (anger when another driver cuts you off, frustration when your partner leaves food out, a canceled client that complicates your schedule, etc.), then apply the muscle of letting go with realizing the unimportance of the matter in the larger scheme of things. In other words, see it from God's perspective, thru His eyes versus your own. As humans we form strong attachments. It is natural that we feel loss so deeply. That is our pendulum, reflected in the constantly shifting and varying nature of life. Let the pendulum swing to the other perspective. This will bring you to a state of neutrality regarding the issue. Is it really that important in the overall view of my life? Everything happens for your highest good, and good comes from every one of life's experiences... look for it, ask for it to be shown.

- Think of consciousness as the gap that happens at the top of the breath when you breathe in. When you breathe out, there's also a gap at the bottom of it. It is within these gaps that everything resides. The action of the breath is a movement. When you access that gap, you are better able to connect with and neutralize your consciousness, which creates resilience to whatever challenge you meet.

- You can access the gap by following a practice or process. It can be something as simple as waking in the morning, sitting on the corner of the bed and straightening your spine. In doing so, you will cause a conscious physiological, chemical and biochemical reaction in your body. Take a couple of deep breaths, and using the power of the mind, set in place your intentions for the day and how it will unfold. See how you are going to manifest your day. The more you do this the more powerful it will become, and you will eventually get to a space whereby you will manifest what you want, rather than what you don't want.

- Shift negative to positive: Everything that has happened, is happening, and will happen to you, comes as it is meant to. Try to see opportunity in every event and situation. It's arrived not to hurt you, but to wake you up. It could be a catalyst for change, for reflection, for letting go. When it feels as though your boat is burning, look at it as a message that it is time to learn how to swim. Once you are on that journey – whether you think you made a choice for it or not – realize it will take you somewhere else and that there's joy in the inevitability of change. Loss can be painful but a new space has opened. You can make a conscious decision to see life from this perspective.

- Explore the consciousness of lack vs. abundance. We all act from our consciousness, whatever it is at any given moment. What is the consciousness of abundance? What is the consciousness of lack? We draw in the elements that reflect our consciousness. When you are operating from a place of abundance, you gather more abundance. The same is true with lack. It becomes what is familiar and comfortable, no matter how much you want to affect change in your life. Fear is the root cause of the consciousness of lack. Think about how fear – that has you feeling you're in defeat before you've even tried – may be blocking your potential.

- Think about making conscious choices in your life that will be positive. You know that exercise, eating healthy, and connecting with nature will feel good, though the motivation to do so could feel like an avoidable task. Make a point of rewarding yourself by consciously remembering the end result. Focus on the company you keep. Are you spending time with people who are positive and reinforce your growth and self-worth? Do you allow negativity into your life because it feels familiar? If you keep it up, you are not using the powers of your consciousness to make a choice. If someone is being unloving, and you keep listening to them again and again, you are gaining negative karma. Look into the subconscious reasons you persist with this pattern and switch your consciousness to self-care by saying, "If you don't have anything loving to say, I have to remove from myself from this friendship/relationship." Though we can tap into all kinds of external help in life, ultimately you must look out for yourself. Your consciousness is your partner in the journey.

- Be aware of your emotions. When anger or depression arises, consciously name it. Avoid reacting or making a big decision until you have processed your feeling and become aware of the who, what, where and why of it. This is especially important in our love, friendship and family relationships.

- Implement a gratitude practice into your life. Gratitude teaches us to live with consciousness and purpose. Make a list, express gratitude to loved ones, keep perspective of your challenges in relation to what others in the world are facing, and be of service to others whenever possible. When you are grateful for your life, you have a greater understanding of it and you're able to look at its complexities in a more neutral light.

- Seek out more information on the topic of consciousness, whether it be the Bhagavad Gita, other teachings and writings, meditations and/or workshops. Every spiritual path and culture has explored consciousness, for our mind is the most powerful force in what it means to be human. It has influenced our histories, our beliefs, our stories and our energy. Consciousness guides our life and our understanding of it.

ABOUT THE AUTHOR

Fondly referred to as the Celtic Sage, Irish-born spiritual teacher Derek O'Neill inspires and uplifts people from all walks of life, offering guidance to influential world leaders, businesses, celebrities, athletes and everyday people alike. Distilled from his life work in psychotherapy, a martial arts career and study with wise yogis and Indian and Tibetan masters, Derek translates ancient wisdom into modern day teachings to address the biggest challenges facing humanity today.

For more than 30 years, Derek O'Neill has been transforming the lives of thousands of people around the world through workshops, consultations, speaking engagements, media, and tireless humanitarian work.

Drawing on years of training in martial arts, which earned him the level of Master

Black Belt, coupled with his extraordinary intuitive abilities and expertise as a psychotherapist, Derek has pioneered a new psychology, transformational therapy. His signature process, aptly named "The Sword and the Brush," helps clients to seamlessly transmute their struggles into positive outcomes, using the sword to cut away old patterns and the brush to help paint the picture of the new life that they require.

Inspired by his worldly travels, Derek and his late wife Linda formed SQ Foundation, a not-for-profit organization focused on helping to solve global issues facing humanity today. In recognition of his service, Derek was honored with the highly prestigious Variety International Humanitarian Award, Arts for India Dayawati Modi Global Award, Irish Autism Action Man of the Year, and Hearts and Minds Pride of Eireann. Derek currently serves on the Board of Directors at Variety International.

Author of More Truth Will Set You Free, the Get a Grip series of pocket books, a cutting edge book on parenting titled Calm Mama, Happy Baby, and several children's books, Derek also hosted his own radio show, "The Way With Derek O'Neill," which enjoyed the most successful launch in VoiceAmerica's history, quickly garnering 100,000 listeners.

To learn more about Derek O'Neill, to attend his next workshops, to order books, download teachings, or to contact him, please visit his website: **derekoneill.com**

To learn more about SQ Foundation, the global charity that is changing the lives of hundreds of thousands of people around the world, go to: **sq-foundation.org**

RESOURCES

'Get a Grip' Book Series
Abundance: Starts Right Now
Addiction: What a Cover-Up!
Anger: Who Gives a Shite?
Bullying: You Won't Beat Me
Confidence: Easy For You to Say
Consciousness: It's All Over You
Depression: What's that?
Desire: Never Fulfilled but Grows
Dreams: The Best Messengers
Excellence: You Never Lost It, You Forgot It
Fear: A Powerful Illusion
Forgiveness: So I Can Move On
Gratitude: Yes Please
Grief: Mind Boggling But Natural
Happiness: You Must Be Effin' Joking!
Love/Divorce: Soulmate or Cellmate?
Mindfulness: Out Of Or In Your Mind?
Relationships: Would You Want to Date You?
Stress: Is Stress Stressing You Out?
Suicide: Fast or Slow
Weight: What's Eating You?

Other Books
More Truth Will Set You Free
Calm Mama, Happy Baby

Children's Books
Water Drop Coloring Book
The Adventures of Lucinda in Love-Filled Fairyland

CONNECT

Visit derekoneill.com for more information.

YouTube
youtube.com/DerekONeill101

Facebook
facebook.com/DerekONeill101

Twitter
twitter.com/DerekONeill101

LinkedIn
linkedin.com/in/DerekONeill101